MORE
MORGAN

MORE MORGAN

A Pictorial History of the Morgan Sports Car

Gregory Houston Bowden

DODD, MEAD & COMPANY
NEW YORK

Published in the United States of America 1977
by Dodd, Mead & Company, Inc.
First published in Great Britain 1976 by Wilton House Gentry, Limited

ISBN: 0-396-07418-9
Library of Congress Catalog Card Number: 76-44655
Printed in Great Britain

Acknowledgments

I am tremendously indebted to Brian Watts whose advice and encouragement throughout the project was invaluable. I am also deeply grateful for permission to reproduce photographs from the outstanding collections of the following, all of whom must be regarded as great scholars of Morgan history: Jake Alderson, Barry Davison, Dennis Rushton, Brian Watts and Colin Wilson.

I am also indebted to the following for their help in supplying information and photographic material: Chris Alford, Chris Booth, John Britten, Chris Cooke, Guy Cox, Tim Cree, Douggie Douglas, Robin Gray, Chris Lawrence, Geoff Margetts, Ray Meredith, Peter Morgan, The Morgan Motor Company, John Orton, John Rowland, Cyril Smedley, Dixon Smith and William Steel.

I would also like to thank Don Jellyman for his inspired cartoons (many of which were produced specially for this book) and also for the endpapers.

I would also like to thank Mr. Norman Lilley of Queensway Photographic Services, Thame, for his noble efforts in processing all the black-and-white photographs so ably and so promptly.

Finally, I would like to thank the following clubs and club officials for their generous help and co-operation:

The Morgan Three-Wheeler Club: Neville Lear and Leslie Reynolds
The Morgan Sports Car Club: Chas. Smith and Cecilia Jellyman
The Morgan Three-Wheeler Club (U.S.A.): John M. Leavens and L. L. McCann
The Morgan Car Club, Washington D.C.: Ed Zielinski and John H. Sheally II
The Morgan Owners' Club of Australia: Val Cross
Morgan-Club Deutschland: Hansjurgen Bell and Reiner Wandert
Morgan Sports Car Club, Holland: A.C. Kentgens-Nijhuis
Morgan Owners' Group, Sweden: Arne Holmstrom
Morgan Sports Car Club, France: Patrick Boisvieux

Contents

Three-wheelers

Contents–*continued*

Four·wheelers

Foreword

Many Morgan lovers like to build up collections of photographs. During the past several months, I have visited a large number of such people and have looked through several thousand pictures. The task was, naturally, a delightful one, and it is from these collections that I have selected the majority of the illustrations which appear in the book. My purpose in compiling this book has been to give everyone interested in the marque the opportunity to own a fine collection of pictures. Above all, my aim has been to give pleasure, rather than provide a work of reference—in other words, to produce something that people will enjoy browsing through time and again. Those who seek detailed information on the history of the marque will find it in the companion volume, *Morgan: First and Last of the Real Sports Cars*.

G.H.B.
Thame, 1976.

Some Early Racers

E. B. Ware at Brooklands in 1913, at the start of a record attempt in his JAP-powered special Morgan. That Ware usually did break the records he attempted undoubtedly has something to do with the fact that he was the head of the experimental department at J. A. Prestwich engines.
(Wilson Collection)

Dignity and—— Turner's Morgan.

(*Above*) This cartoon was drawn in 1926 after a Morgan driven by Joe Turner overtook a Hispano Suiza in a race. The Hispano, which cost ten times the price of the Morgan, broke down a few times after being overtaken. The repairs cost as much as a new Morgan. Joe Turner won a gold medal and covered 67·8 miles in the hour.
(*Alderson Collection*)

(*Top left*) W. D. Hawkes at Brooklands in 1921, in his special racer known as the *Land Crab*. The car was fitted with an MAG engine. Some years later Hawkes joined forces with Gwenda Stewart. As her mechanic, he prepared the cars in which she took so many records in the late twenties and early thirties. They were eventually married.
(*Wilson Collection*)

(*Bottom left*) Robin Jackson raced this car rather successfully at Brooklands in the late twenties. It was then sold to the distinguished Morgan racing driver Clive Lones. The picture was taken in 1930 at Hagley, near Birmingham, where Lones was living at the time, and shows watch-chain fobs and trophies that he had won in this and other cars.

Quite soon after this picture was taken, Lones took possession of a new Morgan, which had been specially built for him, and passed the car on to his wife. Mrs Lones found her car difficult to start, but as the age of chivalry was still alive in the thirties, she was usually able to find someone to help her.
(*MTWC Library*)

15

E. B. Ware his 740-cc JAP-engined Morgan racer. This car has been described
as being in effect just a chassis with half an inverted bathtub on it. Nevertheless,
it was very successful. On this occasion, Ware won the three-lap Cyclecar
Handicap at the British Motor Cycle Racing Club's Brooklands meeting on
4th April 1916. His speed was 54·9 mph.
(Davison Collection)

From the Family Album...

H. F. S. Morgan and his bride, Ruth, leaving for their honeymoon from Ruth's father's vicarage in Malvern. Immediately behind the car is Geoffrey Day—a director of Morgans—and beyond him, almost obscured, is H. F. S.'s father-in-law.
(*Alderson Collection*)

H. F. S. in October 1887—a photograph taken from his sister Dorothy's album.
(Alderson Collection)

(Right) Caricature of H. F. S. from the *Junior Car Club Gazette*. Note the little Morgans under his arms. At this time the JCC was complaining that H. F. S. was not taking sufficient interest in their competitive events and was urging him to do something about it.
(Alderson Collection)

(Below) This famous Morgan was the standard two-seater owned by John Alfred Prestwich, the founder of JAP engines.
(Alderson Collection)

H. F. S. Morgan congratulating Mrs. Clive Lones after she and her husband
had won a 200-mile race. The boy in the schoolcap is Peter Morgan.
(Wilson Collection)

Salute to McMinnies

W. G. McMinnies epitomised the spirit of the early racing Morganists and achieved immortal fame by winning the 1913 Cyclecar Grand Prix at Amiens in France, against some pretty formidable opposition.

McMinnies, who was very shy, somewhat reluctantly agreed to have this picture taken a few moments after climbing out of his car at the end of the 1913 Grand Prix at Amiens. Already his pipe (which always amused the French journalists) is in his hand. Behind him is the tent which the Cyclecar Club had erected for the benefit of English visitors. *(Alderson Collection)*

(Left) The cover of the menu for the dinner given by the Cyclecar Club to McMinnies and his mechanic, Frank Thomas, to celebrate their triumph. Many of the most exciting moments of the race are shown here. Starting in the top left corner and moving clockwise they are as follows: the start; McMinnies taking to the grass to pass Bedelia No. 13 (the car that finished second); the moment when he reluctantly had to face the cameras after the race; the moment of victory; and the tricky business of changing the tube when a tyre burst early in the race.
(Alderson Collection)

(Right) The Cyclecar Club and Frascati's Restaurant evidently had some fun in naming the various courses served on that occasion. At the bottom is another picture of McMinnies taking to the grass to pass Bedelia No. 13.
(Alderson Collection)

McMinnies in action the following year, taking part in the 1914 ACU Six Days
Trial which was based on Sheffield. Here he is seen in his single-seater Morgan
which he called the *Jabberwock* (although he had had an earlier car with the
same name). This was in fact the car he had used in the previous year's Grand
Prix, but with a new body. The old body had been written off in a crash in
August 1913. The engine is a 90-bore JAP.
(Alderson Collection)

A Look at Some Engines

Morgans have never made their own engines. With the exception of the F-type which had a four-cylinder engine, all the three-wheelers had V-twin engines mounted at the very front of the car. The fact that the engine was so accessible and was mounted by such a simple means meant that Morgans could within reason use whatever engines happened to be available at any particular moment. This was especially useful at such times as the period immediately following the First World War, when supplies of engines were very short. Many different kinds of engines were used over the years. Here are a few examples:

Blackburne

(Top) A 1098-cc KMC Blackburne racing engine dating from about 1924, which was run very succesfully at Brooklands by R. T. Horton. Rumour has it that Harold Beart, another celebrated Morganist, used it before it was fitted to Horton's car. Beart took the flying mile record of 1925 at 102·65 mph.
(Watts Collection)

(Bottom) The KMC Blackburne engine in position on the Horton car. Note the downward bend in the bottom cross-tube of the suspension. The story of how this design feature came to be incorporated in racing three-wheelers is a real Morgan classic:

One day in 1927, Clive Lones broke a tie bar whilst racing at Brooklands. He decided to continue racing and the pounding the chassis received caused the engine to drop somewhat. H. F. S. was watching the race and noticed that the more the engine dropped, the better the car was able to corner. Within a few weeks he began to produce cars with pre-bent cross tubes and the new feature was hailed as a great success.
(Watts Collection)

A Look at Some Engines

(Left) Two views of a 1098-cc water-cooled ohv Blackburne of 1926, mounted on a two-speed Aero model. Note the levers which engage with flanges on the push rods. When operated by cable, these levers lift the exhaust valves to reduce compression when turning the starting handle.

This machine is still capable of covering a quarter mile from a standing start in only twenty seconds. In fact, the main reason why Blackburne engines were not more widely used on Morgans was their high cost.
(John Rowland)

JAP

Far more JAP engines were used on Morgans than any other make. When the association between the two companies came to an end in 1933, it marked the end of a quarter of a century of trading.

(Below) This picture shows a brand new Super Sports of 1932 with its factory label still attached. The engine is a 60° LTOWZ (L=series, T=twin, O=overhead valves, W=water-cooled, Z=dry sump).
(Davison Collection)

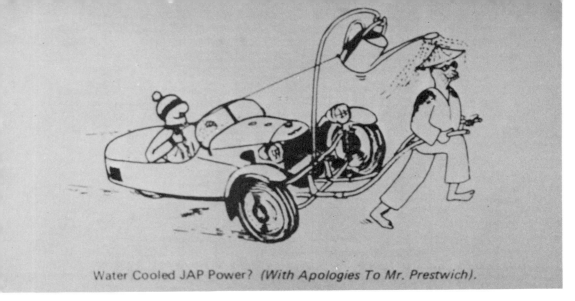

Water Cooled JAP Power? (With Apologies To Mr. Prestwich).

(Above) (MTWC)

A Look at Some Engines

(Bottom left) Another 60° engine of about 1932. This one has a water-heated manifold and is unusual in having a modified starting tunnel in front. Moreover this engine has a magneto, although it would usually have had coil ignition.
(Davison Collection)

Anzani

(Below) An Anzani engine of 1927 with a peculiar valve gear. The valve stems are in two parts, the top half ending in a stirrup shape. The rocker arm works between the two sides of the stirrup with the spring above it.

These engines, which were specially built for Morgans and consequently have a Morgan number stamped on them, are extremely rare. Only about twenty were ever produced and this one, which belongs to Colin Wilson, may be the last one left. It still runs perfectly.
(Wilson Collection)

Another very rare ohv Anzani engine dating from about 1928. Relatively few Morgans were made with Anzani engines—though their distinguished owners included the Duke of York.
(John Rowland)

Matchless

(Right) It was probably only because Morgans were receiving a large number of four-cylinder Ford engines for the F-type that Matchless were able to keep up with the demand for V-twin power units from 1935–9. This engine, the air-cooled ohv MX2 and its successors of 990-cc capacity, was fitted to Super Sports models throughout those years.
(John Rowland)

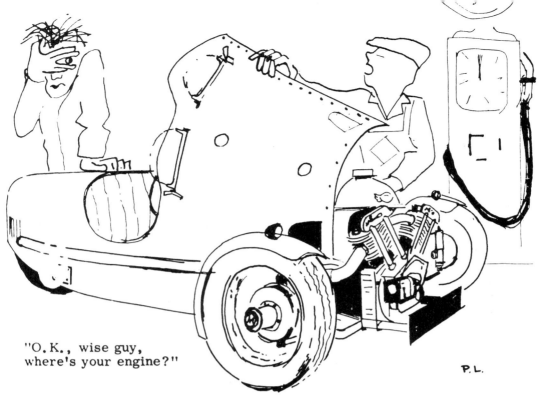

"O.K., wise guy,
where's your engine?"

P.L.

(Above) (MTWC)

If it's
SHEER PERFORMANCE
You Want...
HIGH MAXIMUM SPEED ...
BREATH TAKING ACCELERATION ...
& HIGH SPEED HILL CLIMBING

Make it a
MATCHLESS ENGINED MORGAN
MATCHLESS

All Twin Cylinder Morgans are fitted with Matchless
engines specially designed and built in the famous
Matchless Motorcycle factory for the Morgan Motor
Co. Ltd. These engines combine reliability, durability
and silence with tremendous power output in a
unique degree. There are Water-cooled S.V., Air-cooled
O.H.V. and Water-cooled O.H.V. models from which
to choose.

Advertisement of The Morgan
Motor Co. Ltd. and Matchless
Motorcycles (Colliers) Ltd.

(Left) A Matchless advertisement of 1934. In early 1933
Morgans used a water-cooled,
side-valve Matchless which was
replaced later in the year by the
MX2. The latter was air-cooled
and had overhead valves. At the
end of the year this in turn was
supplemented by the MX4 with
forked conrods and improved
performance.
(Watts Collection)

A 1928 Super Sports Aero modified according to the racing formula of the Morgan Three-Wheeler Club (i.e. with lowered suspension and body). The engine is a side-valve air-cooled JAP KTR. Like all Morgan three-wheelers made before 1932, this car has only two forward speeds and no reverse. It has been very successfully raced all over Europe in recent years, both with this engine and with the more powerful overhead-valve JAP JTO engine. (*Barry Davison*)

A nostalgic sight: 1928 Standard model in County Kerry during the 1975 Irish
National Vintage Rally. This is a rare chance to see the machine in something
like a typical setting of its period: in the twenties, most roads were as peaceful as
this one. A total of one dozen Morgan three-wheelers took part in this rally.
(Barry Davison)

A Matchless MX2 on a 1935 Super Sports. As the engine is air-cooled, the radiator is of course a dummy. The mascot on this particular car comes from a Guy lorry, the 'Indian Chief'. The motto inscribed is 'Feathers in our cap'. *(John Rowland)*

Chassis and Woodwork

Although most three-wheeler owners sooner or later undertake major rebuilding operations and thus find out what their cars look like when undressed, the rest of the world rarely has the chance to see the chassis and bare woodwork.

(Right) Front and rear views of woodwork for a 1928 Super Sports Aero built by Barry Davison.
(Barry Davison)

(Below) Chassis of 1928 Standard model with 50° side-valve JAP engine. The Standard chassis of that period was 6 ins shorter than the Family or Aero.
(Barry Davison)

(*Above*) After a serious crash Clarrie Coombes had to rebuild the chassis of his 1948 F-super completely. He persuaded the man who operated a press brake in his factory (a machine for bending thick sheets of steel) to bend up a new Morgan chassis for him out of 16-guage scrap steel. The result was a great success.
(*Brian Watts*)

(*Top left*) Chassis of 1933 Super Sports beetleback with 990-cc water-cooled side-valve Matchless engine. This is not the original engine: the owner, John Rowland, is preparing an authentic JAP of the period for the car. The steering column on this car has been made self-supporting although it was originally supported from the bodywork. The purists will doubtless object, but there can be no doubt that it was only for reasons of economy that Morgans failed to do this at the time.
(*John Rowland*)

(*Bottom left*) The chassis, wooden sub-frame and skirt panel of the famous Henry Laird 'Red' racing Morgan whilst being rebuilt in the USA by its present owner Vic Hyde. The car is a much modified Super Sports of 1932.
(*Watts Collection*)

37

Two views of the woodwork for a 1948 F-Super rebuilt by Clarrie Coombes.
(*Brian Watts*)

Running Repairs and Restoration

One of the marvels of the Morgan three-wheeler is that it is astonishingly easy for the enterprising owner to carry out even major repairs under extremely difficult conditions. It is happening all the time:

In June 1975 Graham Chivrall was driving his 1914 TT replica, with JAP KT 980-cc air-cooled side-valve engine, on the lower slopes of Hard Knott Pass in the Lake District. He had the misfortune to collide with a rock, fracturing a steering arm. Despite the serious nature of the damage, the car was on the road again within two hours.
(John Rowland)

In the first race of the day at Cadwell Park in 1975, the flywheel of Charles Reynolds' 1000-cc KTOR JAP came off the rear mainshaft. Before the next race had begun, the engine had been removed and the flywheel heated up on a fire of grass and petrol to a temperature at which it was possible to slide it back on to its taper. The job was a complete success and the car ran perfectly for the rest of the day.
(*John Rowland*)

(*Top right*) The remarkably swift manufacture of a push-rod at Silverstone in 1966. Garry Caroline came in for a pit stop having shed a push rod. The total time taken to make and fit a replacement was 9 mins. Caroline re-entered the race—a thirty-minute time trial—and was trying so hard to make up for lost time that he set up a new record.
(*Wilson Collection*)

(*Bottom right*) This Morgan suffered a broken mainshaft in the 1958 Malvern rally organised by the MTWC. Fortunately, among those attending the meeting was Mr. Acock of Bowman and Acock, the Morgan agents in Malvern. He was able to slip off to his stores where he found a new mainshaft and the car was going again later that afternoon.
(*Brian Watts*)

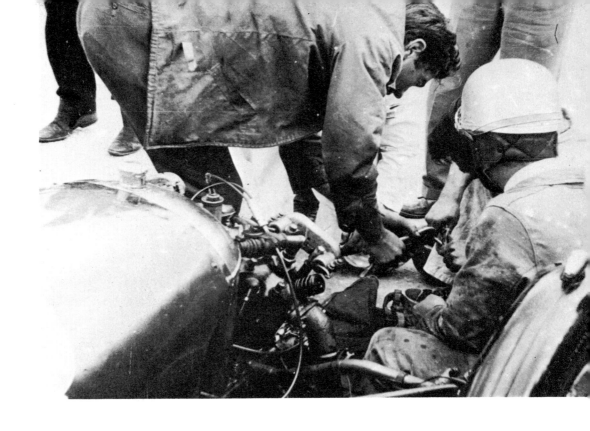

A typical Morgan lover's front room: in this case at the London home of Barry Davison.
(Barry Davison)

'A non-Morganeering sister's view of Morganeering.'
(Barry Davison)

(Right) Vic Hyde's garage in Niles Michigan, USA, whilst he was restoring the Henry Laird 'Red' racer.
(Watts Collection)

(Below) Some members of the MTWC claim that few jobs are impossible so long as you have a good hammer.
(Barry Davison)

Morgan: a suitable case for treatment, or in this case, the restorer's dream. This 1938 Matchless-engined Super Sports was laid up for the war following a de-coke in 1940. It was completely forgotten until 1969 when it was rediscovered with a grand total of 1,444 on the clock. It has since been beautifully restored and now lives with John Leavens in the USA.
(*Davison Collection*)

Catalogues and Posters

The prototype of the 1931 Family model. After very heavy retouching, this photograph was used in the catalogue of that year: because of the rush to produce the catalogue the car had to be photographed before it was finished. The driver is Harry Jones, a director of Morgans, and his three passengers were all members of the company's office staff.

This model was powered by a side-valve JAP.

(Alderson Collection)

Very few posters were ever produced by Morgans. This one dates from 1929 and was also used as a catalogue front at that time.
(Chris Booth)

The art deco style of the 1932 catalogue.
(*Chris Booth*)

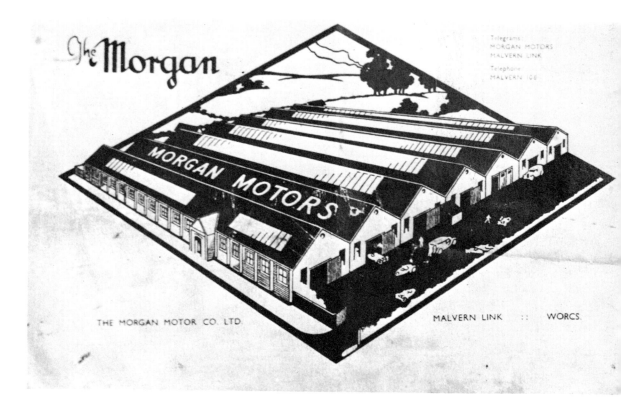

(Above) An artist's impression of the Morgan factory from a 1935 catalogue.
(Douggie Douglas)

(Right) The front of the 1934 catalogue. An artist's impression of a Super Sports with Malvern in the background and the Malvern Hills on the horizon.
(Douggie Douglas)

(*Above*) Front of 1937 catalogue showing the F2. The car has a two-tone finish, such as was very popular at the time. The F-type was introduced in 1933. (*Douggie Douglas*)

Bugatti Owners Club
& Ferrari Owners Club present
MORGAN
60ᵀᴴ ANNIVERSARY
Speed Hill Climb
Concours - Cavalcade
Sunday June 7th 1970 at
PRESCOTT

Co-promoters-
Morgan 4/4 Club. Morgan 3 Wheeler Club.

(*Above*) This poster was in current use in 1974 in St. Tropez at the motor-cycle hire shop. Unfortunately no Morgans were available for hire!

(*Left*) 'It must have been the largest number of Morgan cars ever assembled in one place' was how Peter Morgan described the 60th Anniversary Meeting at Prescott in June 1970. The event drew over ninety three-wheelers and innumerable four-wheelers. It seems that the printers missed out a rather vital part of the car on the poster: it is difficult to understand how the right-hand front wheel is supported! This event was in fact a double anniversary since the MTWC celebrated its 25th birthday at the same time.
(*Douggie Douglas*)

Darmont Morgans

The French never forgot W. G. McMinnies' triumph at Amiens in 1913 and this was undoubtedly one of the factors which encouraged the Paris firm of Darmont and Badelogue to contact H. F. S. Morgan just after the First World War. They expressed the wish to build Morgans in Paris under licence. By 1919 the deal had been concluded and production was in full swing. They sold extremely well during the 1920s and built up quite a track record for themselves. The exact date at which their operation ceased is unknown but it was probably in the late 1920s. Morgans made a further licensing agreement in 1936 enabling Sandford to manufacture 4/4s in Paris.

A corner of the Darmont works near Paris in 1924.

A 1922 Darmont Morgan from the
Bonnal Collection.
(Editions Yvon, Paris)

A Darmont-Morgan fitted with a supercharged twin-magneto Blackburne
engine. The photograph was taken in October 1928. The driver is R. N.
Stewart, Gwenda Stewart's husband. The spectators are evidently impressed
by the high level of decibels generated by the engine!
(Alderson Collection)

From an early Darmont Catalogue.
(MWTC Library)

Le MORGAN RUNABOUT a été présenté au public il y a 15 ans. C'est au Salon de l'Olympia, en 1909, qu'il a fait sa première apparition et, depuis ce moment, il a prouvé ses grandes qualités de résistance dans tous les concours publics les plus importants.

Il a par ce fait un grand avantage sur des véhicules qui n'ont pas encore obtenu de succès et dont les essais n'ont pas été probants.

Ce cyclecar a été construit pour satisfaire aux besoins de ceux qui désirent quelque chose de meilleur marché et de plus simple qu'une voiture, mais aussi quelque chose de plus confortable qu'une motocyclette. Pour atteindre ce but, une attention particulière a été portée sur la simplicité de construction, sur l'accessibilité parfaite de tous les organes, sur la légèreté et aussi la solidité.

Le prix de ce véhicule a été déterminé pour convenir aux personnes de moyens réduits, mais la qualité n'a pas été sacrifiée au bon marché.

SPORTING

Véhicule utilitaire par excellence, très apte au grand tourisme économique.
80 kilomètres à l'heure et 5 litres aux 100 kilomètres.

CARACTÉRISTIQUES

Moteur 10 HP., 2 cylindres en V, nombre de tours : 2.350.

Refroidissement par air ou par eau, suivant demande.

Allumage par magnéto haute tension.

Carburateur automatique avec levier de correction d'air.

Embrayage cône bronze garni de cuir.

Transmission par cardan.

Changement de vitesse donnant 2 vitesses à l'aide de 2 chaînes sur pignons différents.

Châssis breveté en tube d'une résistance incomparable.

Suspension par 2 demi-ressorts à l'arrière et par ressorts à boudin et shock absorbers à l'avant.

Poids : 300 kilos.

Voie : 1 m. 20; empattement : 2 m. 10.

Graissage automatique.

Advertisements

Of all the hundreds of different advertisements published over the years, it has been very difficult to choose which ones should be published here. As *Morgan: First and Last of the Real Sports Cars* included a number of interesting examples from the early years, these are drawn from the twenties and thirties.

(Right) An advertisement dating from December 1923. Although almost all records of Morgan exports during the inter-war years have been lost, advertisements like this one show that the cars were finding their way into numerous foreign countries after the First World War.
(Alderson Collection)

Morgan Runabout

10 PS
wassergekühlt
2 Zylinder, Viertakt-
Blackburne- oder J.A.P.-Motor

Billige Anschaffung,
hohe Leistung

1 Jahr Garantie

☆

Erich Sommaruga, Meyer & Co.
Wien, IV. Karlsplatz 7 (Verkaufshallen)
Telephon 51-2-80/82   Telegramm-Adresse: „Morgbruff Wien"

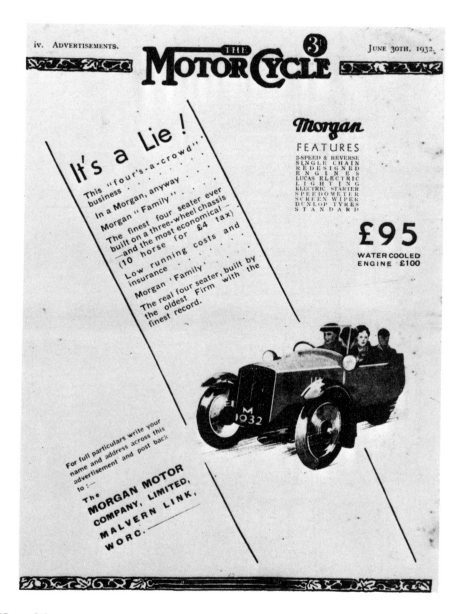

iv. ADVERTISEMENTS.

THE MOTOR CYCLE 3¹

JUNE 30TH, 1932.

It's a Lie!

This "four's-a-crowd" business in a Morgan, anyway

Morgan "Family" . . .

The finest four seater ever built on a three-wheel chassis —and the most economical— (10 horse for £4 tax)

Low running costs and insurance . . .

Morgan 'Family' . . .

The real four seater, built by the oldest Firm with the finest record.

For full particulars write your name and address across this advertisement and post back to :—

The **MORGAN MOTOR COMPANY, LIMITED, MALVERN LINK, WORC.**

Morgan

FEATURES

3-SPEED & REVERSE
SINGLE CHAIN
REDESIGNED
ENGINES
LUCAS ELECTRIC
LIGHTING
ELECTRIC STARTER
SPEEDOMETER
SCREEN WIPER
DUNLOP TYRES
STANDARD

£95

WATER COOLED ENGINE £100

Here Morgans were attempting to refute what they claimed to be a false impression. In this case it was the widely expressed opinion that the only people who could fit in the back of the Family model were legless dwarfs. This advertisement dates from June 1932.

(Alderson Collection)

(Below) Although Morgans were always supplied with hoods, they were not that useful. It was difficult to get into the car with the hood up, and almost impossible to put the hood up from inside. Furthermore, the hood restricted vision to such an extent in the early three-wheelers that some people have described it as like driving inside a pillar box. It was to refute this kind of image that Morgans introduced this advertisement in 1925.
(Alderson Collection)

The All Weather

Morgan Runabout

De Luxe MORGAN fitted with double wind screen and side screens.

Price from £117

Other Models from **£95** complete.

MORGAN MOTOR CO., LTD.,
MALVERN

MORGAN FEATURES
3 SPEEDS & REVERSE
SINGLE CHAIN
REDESIGNED ENGINES
LUCAS ELECTRIC LIGHTING
ELECTRIC STARTER
SPEEDOMETER
SCREEN WIPER
PRICES FROM £95

OLYMPIA
STAND 51

We three saw the winter sunrise and heard the world wake round us ......saw the smoke trails curl from sleepy chimneys ......

Chased flying clouds through mist across the mountains...... until, below, the wild Atlantic a living emerald lay. And so hotelwards......to quiet rooms and blazing fires........ to-morrow, home again,......we three.....good company when Morgan makes a third

MORGAN

For further particulars write your name and address across this advertisement and post back to us.

ISSUED BY MORGAN MOTORS LTD., MALVERN LINK.

(*Above*) During the 1930s Morgan advertisements came up with some of the most delightful copy ever written. This is a fine example. (*Guy Cox*)

"Plus fours"

There's a sense of roomy comfort in the very
words themselves – maybe then you'll get an
idea of the comfort "Morgan Family" offers
when we refer to it as the "Plus Four Car"! !

Four people travelling in comfort on "three
wheels" . . . . . cruising along on the merest
whiff of throttle . . . . . That's economy de
luxe, if you like.

And when you think that there's only £4 tax
and the lowest insurance for any three wheel
car of the same power . . . .

Make 1933 your "3" year! ! . . . . . and
make your "3" a MORGAN.

★ WRITE FOR
NEW LIST
DESCRIBING
FULL RANGE
OF MODELS
●
MORGAN
MOTOR CO. LTD.
MALVERN
LINK, WORC.
●

Morgan FEATURES

★ 3 speeds and reverse Single Chain—
Redesigned Engines - Lucas Electric Light-
ing Electric Starter — Cooper Stewart
Speedometer Screen Wiper. Detachable
Wheels and Spare Wheel fitted to all Models,
Dunlop Tyres Standard.

'Multum in parvo'

THE SPIRIT OF THE BIG RACING CAR!

"*Much in little*" correctly sums up
the qualities of this super sports model.
In workmanship, performance and reliability, there is the same care in manufacture and attention to detail that is vitally
necessary to the big racing car.

To know the thrills and comforts of big
car riding, to get the utmost health-giving
pleasure for yourself and passengers on
the road, invest in a Morgan.

Morgan

SUPER SPORTS MODELS
WATER COOLED £137-10
AIR COOLED £127-10

Write for full particulars
MORGAN MOTOR CO., LTD.,
MALVERN LINK   WORCS.

Advertisements

(Top left) It is interesting to see Morgans advertising what they describe as a 'plus four car' in 1933—a full seventeen years before the Plus 4 model was produced.
(Watts Collection)

(Bottom left) Multum in Parvo or Much in Little was the basis of a famous Morgan advertising campaign in the mid-thirties.
(Watts Collection)

(Below) Morgans suddenly decided in the mid-thirties that it was time to stress fully independent suspension as one of the great features of the car. As every Morgan since 1910 had had this feature, it is surprising that more fuss had not been made before.
(Watts Collection)

Each Wheel SELF-ABSORBENT to Road Shock.

INDEPENDENT WHEEL SPRINGING

Have you realised that this desideratum that 4-wheel Car owners have longed for has been the privilege of Morganists for 21 years?

The Morgan system of independent wheel springing gives a riding comfort that must be experienced to be believed.

It ensures the minimum strain on the chassis on the roughest roads... eliminates "jarring" occasioned by pot-holes, gives a road grip that is constant under the most varying conditions and reduces driver-strain to a minimum.

Ask your dealer for a trial run in a MORGAN... and learn to enjoy road unevenness.

MORGAN MOTOR COMPANY Ltd.
MALVERN LINK ———————— WORC.

Keep abreast of the times by reading "Motor Cycling" Advertisements.   A51

An advertisement for the Family model, 1929.
(*Alderson Collection*)

(*Right*) A late advertisement for the V-twin. By the end of 1937 the production of the four-cylinder F-type three-wheeler and of four-wheeler cars had cut back the production of V-twin models to a very modest level, although they were still available until the war.
(*Watts Collection*)

(Left) The success and popularity of the Morgan made other firms anxious to use the car in their advertising. This is one such example. Mr. Maskell was a famous London Morgan agent. His slogan: 'Maskell for Morgans'.
(Watts Collection)

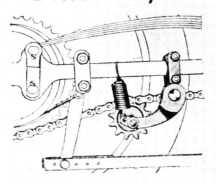

(Right) Outside firms were often anxious to offer accessories to Morgan owners. This item must have seemed very expensive at the time, but well worthwhile because the high speed and low speed chains were not interchangeable (to even out the wear) until 1921.
(Alderson Collection)

This is the only 1928 Standard model still known to exist. The Standard was the cheapest model ever produced by Morgans, its price being £85 10s. It is powered by a side-valve JAP KTC and has direct, ungeared steering. This particular car was one of the last to be built, as the model was dropped later that year. It is also one of the last Morgans to have been built with single-wheel braking. The Standard model is also known as the 'Popular', a name which came about in rather a curious way. At one time, Morgans used poplar in the construction of the sub-frames, and somehow, confusion arose between 'poplar' and 'popular'.
(Barry Davison)

A strange sight at Nurburgring. In August 1974, the Morgan Three-Wheeler Club was invited by the AVD, the German vintage car club, to send a team over to race in Germany. Seventeen cars made the trip, and showed that as well as being a match for other vintage machines, they could give the Ferraris and AC Cobras a run for their money.
(Barry Davison)

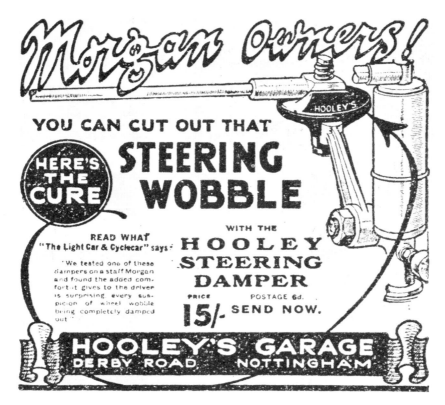

Before opening his own business, Hooley worked for Jack Sylvester, the Nottingham agent for Morgans. That was how he came to know all about the steering wobble problem. The problem existed because early Morgans were not fitted with steering dampers. Enterprising owners would compensate for this by fitting two washers between the joints. Hooley took this idea one step further and then produced his gadget commercially.
(Alderson Collection)

The Factory in the 1920s

With one exception, these pictures come from the Morgan Three-Wheeler Club's Library. The whole set was taken in 1927 and provides a unique opportunity to capture the flavour of the place at that time.

The stores, with Mr. Jay (who became stores manager in 1924) standing in the centre. As in all these photographs, the place has changed astonishingly little since then. Only two or three tyres are kept in each rack today, as modern tyres are so much wider than the 26 x 3½ size then in use. Towards the right-hand side of the picture, note the rods and bands for rear brakes hanging from the beam.

The Machine Shop. Mostly repetitive work on capstan lathes is in progress: e.g., in the lower left-hand corner they are machining sliding axles. The system used by the company was to obtain rough castings of the items they required from subcontractors in Birmingham and then finish them in their own machine shop. The position of Malvern in relation to Birmingham and Oldbury, an area with innumerable small foundries, made this very easy to arrange.

Another view of the machine shop. The man in the foreground is standing at the controls of his milling machine and on the floor nearby is a pile of rear forks which he has milled. In the centre of the picture is a pile of rear hubs—rough castings waiting to be finished.

The body frame assembly shop where wooden parts from the mill were assembled into complete sub-frames.

The blacksmith's shop. The men here are fitting prop shafts onto bevel boxes and assembling other parts of the transmission system. The bevel box castings may be seen on the floor in the centre foreground. Behind them are the cone clutch castings which appear to be complete with linings and thrust bearings.

The frame shop where the chassis were assembled. If you visit the factory today, you can still see these brick hearths in use. You will also see men brazing up Plus-8 frame fronts in an almost identical manner.

The chassis erecting shop where all the various components were fitted onto the basic metal frames. It was here that the chassis complete with bevel boxes were brought to be fitted with wheels, rear forks, chains, brakes, sprockets, prop shafts and engines. By the time the car left here it was a complete Morgan in chassis form. On the right are all the chassis waiting to be completed—this was a space-saving way of keeping them in temporary storage.

Body units complete with radiators in temporary storage, in what is now the repair bay. As much work as possible was completed during the winter months. When the sales period began in April, the work force merely had to fit complete bodies on to complete chassis, and the cars were very soon ready for sale. (This photograph was taken a few years before the others in this chapter.) *(Peter Morgan)*

The trim shop with a Family model centre left and an Aero on either side of it. On the table on the right may be seen the wooden jigs used for making hoods.

The body erecting shop. In the left foreground a Super Sports Aero is nearing completion. A close look at its passenger compartment reveals that it was fitted with a rear-mounted oil tank. This was moved to the front in later models. Notice also the Morgan van, based on the Family chassis, parked half-way down the wall on the left.

The despatch bay, containing a mixture of Family models and Aeros. The Aero at the rear towards the left is fitted with the JAP LTOW engine with overhead valves and camshaft. This engine was introduced in 1926 and was very successful.

The repair bay which, as today, was used both for repairing customers' cars and for fitting certain accessories onto new cars. This department has since moved to a new position, the bay shown in the eighth photograph in this series.

Morgan Vans and Other Freaks

A few Morgan vans were made in the early years, and for a period of about seven years from 1928, they were consistently included in the list of options offered by the company. In a sense they could never have hoped to be enormously successful, because the rear wheel-arch protruded from the floor in the most useful part of the back of the van. Only a few dozen were ever ordered.

A pick-up used by the works for all kinds of odd-jobs before, during and after the First World War.
(Peter Morgan)

Morgan Vans and Other Freaks

(Top left) Pick-ups similar to the one used by the works were available to the public. This one, built in 1913 on a standard chassis, had a carrying capacity of 1¾ cwt (196 lbs or 89 kg) and was known as the Commercial model.
(MTWC Library)

(Bottom left) A rare beast! The works pick-up of the 1930s photographed at Brooklands. Unlike the First World War model, this one is on a three-speed chassis.
(Wilson Collection)

(Below) Not a production model but simply a 1926 Family model which Newman's bakery had had converted into a pick-up for delivering the bread.
(Alderson Collection)

Morgan Vans and Other Freaks

(Left) By the mid-thirties the Morgan van had become far more sophisticated. Mounted on the three-speed Family chassis, it had a carrying capacity of 4 cwt (448 lbs or 204 kg) and rather a smart body. It also offered the driver better weather protection than any other three-wheeler produced at the factory. *(Watts Collection)*

(Below) An experimental vehicle produced at the beginning of the First World War: it was hoped that it would interest the Army. It was designed to carry a machine gun, mounted in the rear and operated by the rear-facing passenger. The Army did not take it up, and this was the only model to be produced. *(Peter Morgan)*

Morgan Vans and Other Freaks

(Above) Reacting to the art-deco flavour of the 1930s, Jack Sylvester, the Nottingham Morgan agent, built this special body out of ash and aluminium. Despite the use of the latter, the total weight of the car was more than 8 cwt (896 lbs or 407 kg) and was thus over the legal weight limit for a three-wheeler. Surprisingly, it only had two seats although there were cushions in the rear space for any extra passengers. After using the car for some time, he dismantled it and sold off the chassis complete with its Crouch gearbox mounted amidships. He adapted the body to fit a Rover 10.
(Alderson Collection)

(Left) The first Morgan with a built-in (or rather built-on) wireless. This was proudly announced in the *Light Car and Cyclecar* in April 1923. The magazine explained: 'Owned by the Stratford Wireless Co., this cyclecar is equipped with two enormous Magnavox loudspeakers. Running fore and aft over the heads of the occupants is a conspicuous sausage-type aerial that gives the vehicle the appearance almost of one that has been rigged for participation in a carnival. . . The wireless receiving set fitted to this vehicle is very efficient in operation and we are informed by its owner that he has heard the Cardiff broadcasting station while the Morgan was in the vicinity of Stratford.' At that time, it was considered essential for all wirelesses to have an earth. Tongue in cheek, the Stratford Wireless Co. mounted an earth-filled flower-pot on the running board and connected the wireless to it.
(Wilson Collection)

In the foreground of this picture, slightly to the left, is the experimental four-wheeler Morgan built in the early part of 1914. It never went into production and no other four-wheeler was built until 1935. The photograph was taken outside the Rectory at Stoke Lacey in Herefordshire, the home of H. F. S. Morgan's father, the Rev. George Morgan.
(Davison Collection)

4.14 THREE-WHEEL SPORTS CAR

Fig. 4.14

From a Meccano catalogue of the mid-thirties.
(Watts Collection)

Morgans and the Law

(Top right) 'Car or motorcycle?' This photograph is a reminder of one of the great controversies which rocked the cyclecar world between the wars. What was the true definition of a cyclecar? The car shown here is a 1926 JAP-engined Aero.
(Alderson Collection)

(Bottom right) Although the law was sometimes chasing Morganists, occasionally the reverse happened too when the law used Morgans to do their chasing.
(Douggie Douglas)

A Morgan powered by two Scott engines joined by Granville Grenfell. The latter was a remarkably inventive and capable engineer who built all kinds of 'specials' at his workshop near Brooklands. This was perhaps one of his slightly less successful efforts since it tended to be front heavy. With so much power available that tended to be a little dangerous!
(*Motor Cycling*)

Odd Angles

Bird's·eye View

1934 three-speeder Super Sports—an example of the 'beetleback' body. The front cap is the oil filler, the rear cap is for petrol. If a triangle is drawn through the three wheels, almost the entire weight of the car will be found centred within that space. This is one of the features which result in superb handling. Notice also the rear louvres which are there just to add a dash of style. (*John Rowland*)

A 1928 two-speeder Super Sports Aero. The hump in the tail was not a feature of the car as it left the factory. It had to be made later when the chassis was lowered for racing.
(Barry Davison)

Bottoms and Rear Views

(Right) Aero of 1925. This particular car was the one regularly loaned by the works to magazines for road tests. The low-level silencers may clearly be seen but unfortunately the rear band brake is somewhat obscured. The spotlamp seen to the left of the driver's hat was an optional extra. Beneath it is located the bulb of the horn.
(Alderson Collection)

View of the paddock at Silverstone in 1967, taken from the scoring tower and showing a mixture of barrelbacks and beetlebacks.
(Colin Wilson)

Sides

(Right) A meeting at Silverstone in 1966. Over twenty three-wheelers were out that day.
(Colin Wilson)

(Left) On the grid at Silverstone in 1969. Drivers top to bottom are Shotten, Duncan, Caroline and Weeks.
(Barry Davison)

Hoods Up

(Above) The normal Morgan lover's hood in action: an umbrella. The photograph was taken at the 1972 MTWC Club Sprint at Gaydon. The car and its owner John Leavens are now back in the USA.
(Barry Davison)

(Left) Now perhaps you understand the problem of getting into a Morgan with the hood up!
(Barry Davison)

The Oddest Angle of All

(Above) Urgent repairs at a Vincent owner's club meeting at Cadwell Park caused Tim Green to prop up his 1930 Super Sports Aero on an old fencing post. This kind of outlandish black and yellow colouring was all the rage at Brooklands between the wars. The car is powered by a JAP KTOR racing engine of 1000-cc designed to run on methanol.
(John Rowland)

(Above) To end this chapter here is an unusual view of the cockpit of Gwenda Stewart's single-seater racing Morgan of 1930. This car, in which she broke innumerable records, was built at the factory in 1930, incorporating many special features devised by Douglas Hawkes. Note the battery of drip feeds enabling her to see at a glance whether oil was being fed to all the essential places, also the central prop shaft and gear lever which she sat astride. On the left is a lever which operated a pump to increase fuel pressure.
(Alderson Collection)

Two-wheeler Morgans?

Despite the superb cornering ability of Morgan three-wheelers, they will eventually drop on to only two wheels if they are pushed too hard. Their very high power to weight ratio makes this all too easy to achieve.

Two-wheeler Morgans?

(Left) John Hooper ascending Blue Hills Mine in the Lands End trial of 1932. His car is a completely standard 1931 Aero, which he used in races and hillclimbs with a good measure of success. In this case he had been told by another driver that his only chance of making this section of the course was to go flat out. Unfortunately his adviser had not realised that flat out for him was a great deal less than flat out for the Morgan. Luckily Hooper suffered only minor damage and was able to continue with the trial. Note his passenger Bertie Le Man's hand on the ground, trying to stop the car tipping over. *(Alderson Collection)*

(Below) A scene from a race at Cadwell Park in the early 1950s. Regrettably no further details are available. The car is a three-speed Super Sports of 1934. *(Colin Wilson)*

Two-wheeler Morgans?

(Top left) The 1928 ex-Horton car at Dyrrham park in the mid-sixties. This car was designed for Brooklands and not for narrow corners like this. *(Photo courtesy Sodbury Gazette)*

(Bottom left) 'The perfect cure for insomnia.' *(MTWC)*

The Antidote

Although the driver, if wearing a heavy gauntlet, can give himself a correcting push on a sharp left-hand bend, by far the most effective way of avoiding rolling over on fast corners is to have a well-trained, agile and extremely brave passenger.

(Below) H. Martin driving a 1074-cc Anzani-engined Morgan in the Southern Counties Cycling Union meeting at Herne Hill in August 1923. Thanks to his passenger's efforts, this car took the mile record in 1 min 35 seconds. *(Wilson Collection)*

Jim Sowden driving a very late F-Super.
(Colin Wilson)

Mike Guess at the Morgan 60th Anniversary meeting at Prescott in 1970. This
is the corner known as Pardon.
(Colin Wilson)

Amphibious Morgans

A very late Aero Morgan driven by Hooper in the London to Edinburgh trial
of 1932.
(Wilson Collection)

The Auto-Cycle Union's six-day trials were always famed for the appalling routes over which they were run. A ford as deep as the one shown in this picture of the 1923 Six Days Trial was in no way unusual, despite the anxious look on the face of the driver, W. Carr. The Morgan is an Anzani-engined Standard model.

(*Davison Collection*)

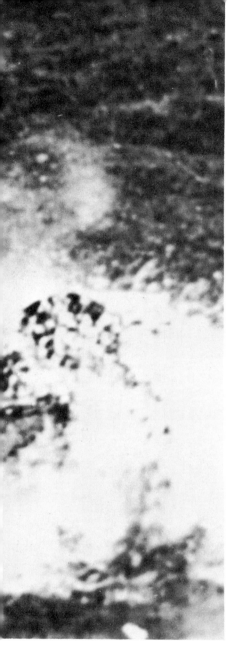

(*Below*) Taken on a trial, the exact details of which are unknown, Jack Sylvester, the Nottingham Morgan agent of the inter-war years, is shown here 'entertaining' the spectators from his Standard model Morgan. In order to have more fun, the spectators had partly blocked the ford and thus raised the water level. Sylvester's passenger may be seen examining the water seeping up through the floor of the car.
(*Alderson Collection*)

(Above) 'I'm not worried if you are getting wet. The Moggie's not staying out in this.'
(MTWC)

(Above) Garry Caroline sitting in a duck pond near Coventry. The nearside front brake failed, causing the car to veer violently to the right, go over a bank and end up in this pond. Garry was unhurt but the car was seriously damaged. *(Colin Wilson)*

(Bottom left) A picture of a Wye Valley Trader's Trial of the early 1930s from George Goodall's album. The two-speeder Morgan is anxiously heading for what appears to be the shallowest part of the stream. *(MTWC Library)*

Morgans in the Snow

No Morgan lover can bear to have his hood up—no, not even when it is snowing.

A race meeting at Croix en Ternois near Arras in France, organised by ASAVE—the French historic vehicle racing club—in April 1975. Three members of the MTWC went over for the race and finished first, second and third. Barry Davison commented afterwards: 'We raced in drifts of snow and had a whale of a time although winning speeds were down to about 40 mph.' The other two Morganists on this occasion were Gregg Bibby and Tony Quinn.
(Barry Davison)

Morgans in the Snow

The Wiborg Wood Co. of Finland use this Morgan daily. In order to make progress over the snow-covered country, the front wheels have been replaced with skis and a chain encircles the rear tyre.

(Alderson Collection)

Frank Gillam leaves his F-Super to turn white at the home of Clarrie Coombes.
(Brian Watts)

Dealers

A glimpse of a typical Morgan dealer's premises in the early twenties. This is
Bennetts of Nottingham and Jack Sylvester may be seen standing centre left. It
was he who set up the cyclecar side of the business. A Grand Prix Morgan and
Beardmore Precision motorcycle are parked outside.
(Alderson Collection)

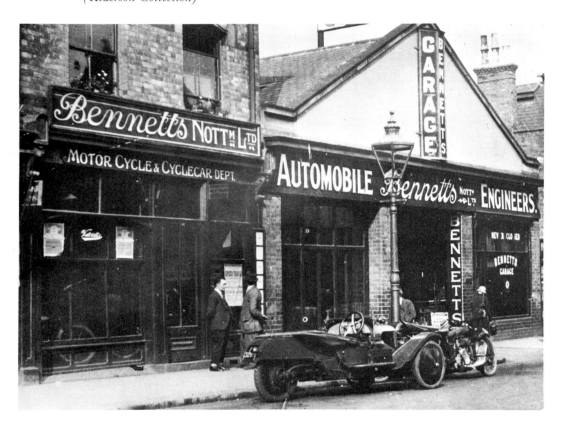

Some Morgan agents gathered outside the Royal Oak at Malvern in 1922, whilst on a visit to the factory to collect new cars. In those days the dealers really believed in making the most of their visits to Malvern and sometimes spent two or three days there—just to collect a car. On the far left at the rear is Billy James of Sheffield. The man on the right in a bowler is thought to be Horrocks, the Bolton agent.

The Morgan Three-wheeler Club

The MTWC was founded in 1945 (although other Morgan clubs had existed before the war) and organises both competitions and social events on a regular basis. In addition to the central organisation, which manufactures spare parts, has a library and technical information service, and publishes a monthly magazine, there are regional groups throughout Britain. Every year there are always two national sprint meetings and the club is frequently invited to race at such places as Silverstone, Mallory Park and Brands Hatch. Recently, an increasing number of invitations to race abroad has been received and eagerly accepted.

(Below) A typical view of the MTWC in action. This was taken at Silverstone in the late sixties.
(Davison Collection)

'Do 'e think there be a circus around here George?'
(*MTWC*)

Clarrie Coombes in an F-4 on the MTWC Primrose Run in 1966. Terling Ford
in Essex offers drivers an expanse of water 18 ins deep and 100 yards wide—a
somewhat daunting prospect. Coombes worked out that he could just fit onto
the pedestrian bridge and thus save himself a two-mile detour. Happily the
bridge was strong enough to support the weight of the car.
(*Brian Watts*)

(Above) At the Nurburgring in Germany, 1974. At the end of the day, a race was held for the fastest twenty cars regardless of engine size, etc. Garry Caroline, driving a 1928 Super Sports Aero, is seen here paralysing MGs and Porsches. Eventually he even passed the AC Cobra in front of him.
(Barry Davison)

(Top left) Part of the festivities for the MTWC's south-east group camping holiday in Norfolk in 1971. Every car in this picture is in regular use—there is no question of 'dusting off the cobwebs' to get ready for an event like this.
(Barry Davison)

(Bottom left) A meeting at Prescott in 1970 provides the opportunity to see four different kinds of engine on Aero models. The 1929 Super Sports Aero on the extreme right belongs to Pete Lovelace and has a 50° JAP; the Aero next to it is Andy Duncan's with a 'dog-eared' JAP; next to that is Andy Parry-Keene's with a Blackburne engine. On the far left is Pete Thompson's Anzani-engined Aero.
(Barry Davison)

(Overleaf) In July 1975 the British Racing and Sports Car Club invited the MTWC to one of its meetings at Mallory Park. On the left is Peter Enticknap in a 1928 Super Sports Aero powered by a KTOR JAP racing engine; No. 12 is Greg Bibby in a 1934 Super Sports with a 50° racing JAP; No. 11 is Barry Davison in a 1928 Super Sports Aero with a JAP air-cooled engine of doubtful vintage; and on the right is Brian Stratford in his 1934 beetleback Super Sports.
(Barry Davison)

A corner of the paddock at Prescott in June 1970 at the famous meeting celebrating the 60th anniversary of the Morgan Motor Co. and the 25th birthday of the MTWC.
(Colin Wilson)

(Top right) One of a series of cartoons by Sylvia Sampson, showing well-known club members and cars.

(Bottom right) Adrian and Tricia Murray-Leslie in their 1172-cc side-valve Ford-powered F-type lead Garry Caroline round a hairpin at Cadwell Park in August 1971. Many people imagine that an F-type can never be a match for the sporting V-twins, but Murray-Leslie has proved them wrong. Since this picture was taken, he has supercharged the car and now gets through a new rear tyre every thousand miles.
(John Rowland)

Three-wheelers in the USA

Since 1970, a branch of the MTWC has been flourishing in the USA. It began when three Morgan owners wrote independently to Alan Lazenby, the chairman of the MTWC, asking for recognition of an American group. The organiser is John Leavens, who operates from his home in Santa Monica, California. Membership hovers around the sixty mark, and those sixty people between them own fifty-five three-wheelers. Leavens estimates that there are between 120 and 150 three-wheeler Morgans in North America. A quarterly newsletter keeps the members in touch with each other and offers technical advice, as well as a useful advertising section for members who wish to buy or sell spare parts. In addition to organising its own events, the group often joins forces with the four-wheeler fraternity, and with motorcycle and vintage car clubs.

The cover of one of the American group's quarterly newsletters.

The Morgan

THREE - WHEELER CLUB

FOURTH QUARTER 1975 NEWSLETTER

Merry Christmas and Happy New Year.

$3 subscription for 1976 is now due!

Vic Hyde with two of his F-types. He has a total of thirty-seven British three-wheelers in his collection.

Larry McCann of the Chicago section of the MTWC with his JAP-powered beetleback. On the right is Joe Pearson's barrelback.

Joe Pearson in touring form.

(Right) Touring the open country of the midwest states in a barrelback JAP.

Vic Hyde in his ex-Laird 'Red' racing Morgan. He was so impatient to try it out that he ignored its (temporary) lack of chassis or engine.

Pearson and Phil Sked at work on Phil's 1934 MX4.

Three-wheelers in the USA

Larry McCann and Brian Kinkaid warming up for some fast laps.

Phil Sked's finished product.

Birth of the 4/4

The photographs in this section all come from the remarkable collection which has been assembled by Dr. Jake Alderson and Mr. Dennis Rushton.

This is the very first 4/4 ever built on a proper 4/4 chassis. The only previous prototype had been built on a modified F-type three-wheeler chassis. This photograph was taken at Brooklands in July 1935 while H. F. S. Morgan was testing the car. Then as now the chassis was made by Rubery-Owen.

(*Above*) The same car after numerous alterations had been effected. It was in this form that the 4/4 went into production. The principal modifications carried out during the time that elapsed between these two photographs are as follows: a proper windscreen substituted for the fly-screens; specially designed front wings (in the earlier version, the same kind of wings had been used on the front as on the rear: although this was economically desirable, it was not very beautiful and the idea was dropped); a purpose-built 4/4 production radiator (the car in the earlier photograph is fitted with a modified three-wheeler radiator). Minor alterations were also carried out on the doors.

(*Top right*) The sad fate that met this most significant prototype: this picture was taken in the factory's repair bay shortly after George Goodall had crashed the car near Hereford. It was never rebuilt.

(*Bottom right*) In the best Morgan tradition, a heavy programme of trials and competitions was arranged for the new model in 1936, so that the public could see for itself what a reliable car this was. Here Harry James, a director of Morgans, is seen driving the prototype up Fingle Bridge—a section of the London to Exeter trial—a few months before the crash.

(Top left) A racing version of the 4/4 built for the RAC Tourist Trophy at Donnington in 1937. Later a small number of replicas were built, known as 4/4 TT Replicas. The car was fitted with flyscreens, cycle-type front wings and an unusual exhaust system which is clearly displayed in this photograph. The building in the background is the small workshop at the circuit which Morgans used for their final preparation work.

(Bottom left) The same car on the starting line. Looking into the bonnet is Charlie Curtis (who was still Morgan's racing mechanic at Le Mans in 1962 and only retired in 1971), with Jim Goodall standing behind him. On the extreme left of the picture is the driver, Henry Laird and the lady bending down beside him is his wife, Barbara.

(Above) Taken from the Morgan pits during the 1937 TT. Unfortunately the car did not do very well as a stub axle broke, causing it to veer off the track. Fortunately there were no injuries.

129

The Morgan 4/4 team at Bude in the 1939 Lands End Trial.

It did not take Morgans very long to produce a four-seater version of the 4/4. However, as no production model was ready at the time the 1936 catalogue had to go to press, it was decided to use an artist's impression superimposed on a background of the Malvern Hills.

The famous Blue Hills Mine near Lands End, during the 1939 trial. This hill is on the side of a quarry and is one of the most popular points for spectators. This 4/4 is being driven by Harry James and his wife, Lola. They are about to attempt the restart: an important test to prove both the power of the car and its ability to grip on a rough road with a very steep gradient. This sort of test has never worried Morgans.

Some Very Rare Models

The 4/4 TT Replica

The 4/4 TT Replica is one of the two rarest kinds of four-wheeler Morgan, the other being the Le Mans Replica. Only six of these machines were ever built and they were designed for the RAC Tourist Trophy race at Donnington in 1937. This particular car was originally the property of Peter Morgan, but by the time this picture was taken it had ceased to be a works car and had become the property of Dixon Smith. He is seen here, driving it in an inter-club trial at Honeybourne, near Evesham in 1956. The original Climax engine was blown up by Jim Goodall on a straight near Malvern, and a Standard 10 Special was therefore substituted.
(*Charles Dunn*)

The Le Mans Replica

The Le Mans Replica was the last Morgan model to be introduced before the war—in February 1939. Four or five of these cars were built during that year, and a further three were built up out of spare parts soon after the end of the war. As its name implies, it was built with Le Mans in mind. Superficially, it resembles the TT Replica, chiefly because of its cycle-type front wings. However, there are a few significant differences:

The section of the tonneau cover behind the seats of the Le Mans car is made of metal; on the TT it is made of canvas. The tonneau also slopes more steeply down towards the rear on the Le Mans model.

The spare wheel on the Le Mans car is almost completely flush with the back of the car. On the TT, it stands proud.

The Le Mans Replica's Coventry Climax engine was fully balanced with polished ports. It had a compression ratio of 8·5:1. The car had Burman steering, Lucas lighting and a Meadows gearbox.

John Orton, registrar of 4/4 Series I models, recently undertook a complete rebuild of his 1946 Le Mans Replica. This provided an excellent opportunity to take a close look at it:

The cycle-type front wings.

The balanced Coventry Climax engine.

Some very rare Models

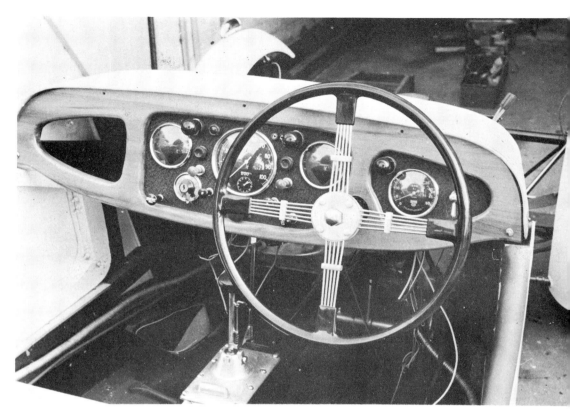

The dashboard and the Meadows gearbox.

The almost flush spare wheel and the sloping metal tonneau cover.

(Above) The Le Mans Replica's back axle.

The 4/4 Drophead Coupé

Although not as rare as the Le Mans or TT Replica, less than fifty 4/4 Drophead Coupés were built. These cars were all produced between 1938 and 1950. The fortunate John Orton is the owner of one of the last ones ever built—a 1950 model in fact. It is a car of exquisite beauty.

(Below) The 10 hp Standard Special engine seen from both sides. This was available from 1938 onwards as an alternative to the Coventry Climax, though it was always used on Drophead Coupés. It is to be found on all four-wheelers made between the end of the war and the winter of 1950. It had a capacity of 1,267 cc and produced 38·8 bhp at 4,800 rpm though it could safely run at 5,500 rpm. The bottom half of the engine was a normal Standard model but the top half was specially made for Morgans—spare cylinder heads are now in very short supply! Note the special rocker cover bearing the Morgan name and the copious supply of spare sparking plugs housed beneath the bonnet.

The construction of the windscreen immediately shows that this is a drophead. Unlike other models, it is built as an integral part of the bodywork.

(*Top right*) For elegant touring, the hood could be fastened in the Sedanca de Ville manner.

(*Bottom right*) The graceful curvature of the rear, the tiny back window and the double spare wheels.

The Plus 4 in transition

This rare Plus 4, built late in 1953 for the Motor Show, is the property of A. J. Smith. It is the very first Morgan built with the modern shaped front and is especially rare because of two features which were dropped early in 1954: (i) the radiator grille is only slightly curved and has a stone guard at the top on which the Morgan badge is mounted; (ii) the headlamps are set in straight tubes and are set straight into the wings. Early in 1954, a change in the law required the headlamps to be higher, and this led to the adoption of the modern shape of headlight tube.

The rear end of the car was scarcely changed at all at the time of the front reshaping, and until 1955, the two-seater models carried twin spare wheels while the four-seaters carried only one.

After the Motor Show of 1955, all four-wheelers carried only one spare wheel and the back ceased to have a double curvature. In its new form, the cowelling over the petrol tank simply had one curve at the top and then went diagonally down.

The car shown here was also the first to be fitted with the Triumph TR2 engine. It was run by the Morgan factory for some time before passing into private hands.

(Fred Scatley)

Modifications to the Plus 4

Unless otherwise stated, changes were introduced at the London Motor Show (normally in October).

1950	Plus 4 introduced. Replaced 4/4 range completely. Available as two-seater, four-seater and Drophead Coupé. Powered by Standard Vanguard engine.
1953	Introduction of cowled front and streamlined headlamps. Introduction of Triumph TR2 engine on models except four-seater Drophead Coupé.
1954 (spring)	Headlamps raised. Stone guard removed from radiator grille.
1955	All models fitted only with single spare wheel. Single curvature on petrol tank cowelling.
1957	Introduction of low radiator cowell. Width of two-seater models increased by 4 inches.
1958 (early)	Width of four-seater models increased by 4 inches. Petrol tank on two-seaters placed down on the chassis so that the petrol tank cowelling lost even its single curve, and the rear panel became a diagonal straight line.
1962	Introduction of Plus 4 Super Sports.
1966	Lower body introduced on all Plus 4 two-seaters.
1969 (early)	Last Plus 4 leaves the factory.

This fully enclosed 2-seater sports car is developed from the successful Morgan Plus Four. It shares with that model, tractability and ease of control, with the added refinements of deep luxurious seating and year-round weather protection.

The Plus Four Plus provides smooth, quiet travel at speeds up to 110 m.p.h. yet remains completely docile and manageable in heavy traffic. It is safely controlled by 11″ dia. front disc and rear drum brakes.

Admire the smooth sweeping lines of the Plus Four Plus, then step into the spacious interior. There's more than ample room for two, in comfort, with luggage space, plus the useful boot. The seating position is low and purposeful, with excellent vision through the deep windscreen and winding windows. Full instrumentation is provided and controls fall easily to hand in the true sports car manner.

Price £1,055 plus p. tax £220 7s. 1d. **£1,275 7s. 1d.**

The Plus 4 Plus

(Left) The Plus 4 Plus was the only non-convertible Morgan to be produced. The car, which had a fibreglass body, would be rather attractive if it were not for the very sharp curve of the roof, which necessitates almost semi-circular side windows. Although it was thought that fifty were made, recent research by Tim Cree has proved that the total production numbered only twenty-six. Unbelievably, the company did not lose any money on this venture.

The Plus 4 four-seater Drophead Coupé

Although two special flat-rad, Plus 4, four-seater Drophead Coupés were made (one of which was H. F. S. Morgan's), the model was only on offer to the general public during 1954 and 1955. A total of forty-seven was produced during this period. They are the only Morgans, apart from the Plus 4 Plus, ever built with what can be described as a normal (if small) boot. These photographs show one of the last cars of this kind to be built. It is the property of Dixon Smith.

(Below) It is quite a surprise to see a Morgan with a boot!
(Charles Smith)

(Above) From the front, the car looks very much the same as the two-seater drophead.
(Charles Smith)

(Right) Unfortunately the spare wheel takes up so much space that there is little room for anything else.

Curious Coachwork

Beautiful though the Morgan body is, people have occasionally been tempted to transform their cars in some strange way. In some cases this has been done as a pure whim, in others for a more practical reason such as the provision of a boot. Here are some examples:

Two views of a 1937 4/4 with an aluminium body built by the famous Granville Grenfell at his workshop near Brooklands. Two of these were produced but only this one survives.
(Colin Wilson)

(Right) This boot conversion was designed by the original owner of this 1952 Plus 4—John Ahern. He was a well-known vintage and veteran motorist, and a committed Morgan lover. The work was carried out by J. Jarvis of Walmer Road, London.
(J. H. Ahern)

(Below) A 4/4 Drophead Coupé of 1939 with an unusual rear end treatment including a fully enclosed spare wheel. Henry Laird used to call this car 'Uncle George's Winter Carriage' which suggests that George Goodall might have been its owner.
(Alderson Collection)

Just after the war, when Morgans were desperately short of materials, they sold a number of cars as rolling chassis, leaving the owner to build a body of his own. This early post-war Series I is one such example. The estate body was built and fitted by a garage in Devon.

Catalogues

While many will doubtless disagree, I find that Morgan's four-wheeler catalogues have been for the most part less attractive than those for the three-wheelers used to be. I have therefore included here only a few which seem to be of special interest.

Earliest Plus 4 catalogue—1950.

From the 1958 catalogue.

1963 catalogue introducing the Plus 4 Plus.

1963/64 Prices for full range of cars	Basic	Purchase Tax	Total
4/4 Series V.1498 c.c Ford engine	£565	£118 · 5 · 5	£683 · 5 · 5
4/4 Series V Competition model	£625	£130 · 15 · 5	£775 · 15 · 5
Plus 4 2-Seater	£675	£141 · 3 · 9	£816 · 3 · 9
Plus 4 4-Seater	£690	£144 · 6 · 3	£834 · 6 · 3
Plus 4 Super Sports	£925	£193 · 5 · 5	£1118 · 5 · 5

(c) The decision of the Company on all claims shall be final and the purchaser agrees to accept its decision on all matters relating to defects and the exchange or replacement of parts.

MORGAN MOTOR CO. LTD.
PICKERSLEIGH ROAD
MALVERN LINK
WORCESTERSHIRE, ENGLAND
Telephone: MALVERN 106.

How is this for nostalgia!

(Right) Charles Morgan's artistic influence may be seen in the art deco catalogue of 1973.

4/4 4 seater

Cubic Capacity—97.6 cu. ins. (1,599cc.)
Bore and Stroke—3.188"×3.060" (81mm×77.62mm)
Compression Ratio—9. 2: 1
B.H.P.—98 at 6,000 rpm.
Torque—100 lb. ft. 13.8 mkg. at 3,600 r.p.m.
Type of Carburettor—Weber Twin Choke 32/36 downdraught
Number of Cylinders—Four
Firing Order—1, 2, 4, 3.
Oil Capacity—7.5 pints (4.25 l.) 7 pints(4 l) refill.
Petrol Capacity—10 gallons, 45.5 litres.

The 4/4 4 seater combines the sporting performance of
the 2 seater with the advantages of a family car. There
is plenty of leg and headroom in the back seat when the
weatherproof hood is raised, a fresh air heater for cold
wintry mornings and opening side windows for all four
passengers.

Advertisements and Posters

The earliest advertisement for the 4/4—late 1935/early 1936.

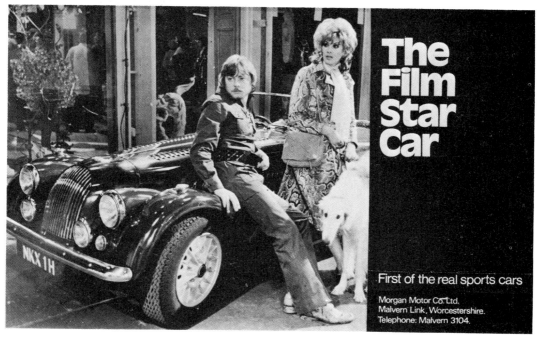

(Above) An advertisement for 1969.

THE LEADER

Morgan Plus 8 £1699·51
Goose-pimple surge of lightweight V8. 0-70 in 7.5.
In-out of corners and over the brow.
This is the Morgan we've always wanted to make,
leader of the range, leader of the pack.
Difficult to find such performance
and safety at the price—some say elegance too.

An early advertisement for the Plus 8. Here Cyril Smedley, who owns the advertising agency used by Morgans, is seen making a lot of smoke in his own Plus 8.

From time to time Morgans receive some free advertising, when the manufacturer of a product uses one of the cars as part of the background for his advertisement. The American Genesee beer company is one such example.

Advertisements and Posters

Sadly, Morgans have produced very few posters during their long history. An extensive search has uncovered only three for the whole four-wheeler period. (The third poster is reproduced in colour.)

(Overleaf) Produced in about 1951.

(Below) Produced in about 1962 and inspired by Chris Lawrence's class win at Le Mans that year.

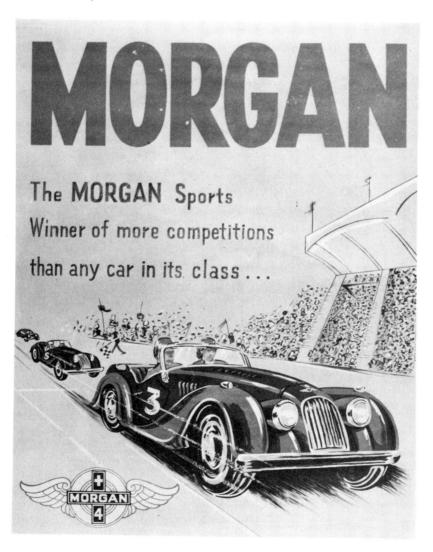

Morgan +4

The Sports Car of Distinction

MORGAN MOTOR CO. LTD. · MALVERN LINK

The 4/4 Revived

The 4/4 disappeared in 1950, when it was replaced by the Plus 4 range. Triumph TR2 engines were always in rather short supply in the early 1950s and Morgans sometimes had difficulty in obtaining enough to keep production moving. It was therefore decided in 1955 to reintroduce an updated 4/4 with a Ford engine, and to produce it in addition to the Plus 4 range. The new 4/4 was known as the Series II. It was equipped with the 10 hp 1172 cc Ford 100E side valve engine and a three-speed Ford gearbox. This provided it with a modest 0–60 acceleration time of 29·6 seconds. Thus the Series II was always regarded more as a touring car than a sports car.

(Below and overleaf) The very first 4/4 Series II. This was a works car which was almost immediately driven to victory in the Taunton National Motorcross by Peter Morgan. It had an Elva cylinder head conversion but was otherwise a standard production model, having drum brakes all round.

(Dixon Smith)

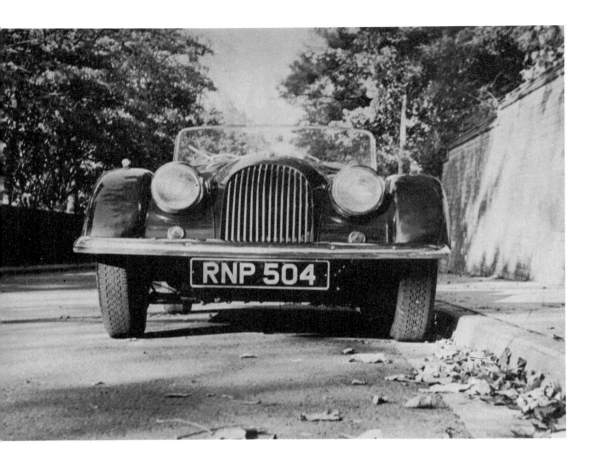

4/4 Models

1935	Prototype 4/4 built.
1936	Climax engined 4/4s in production.
1937	TT Replicas built.
1938	Drophead Coupé available. Standard Special engine available.
1939	Le Mans Replica introduced.
1946-50	All 4/4s fitted with Standard Special engines.
1950	4/4 production dropped.
1955	Introduction of 4/4 Series II. 1172 cc side-valve Ford 100E engine and three-speed gearbox.
1960	Introduction of Series III with Ford 105E engine and four-speed gearbox. This engine (which was used by Ford in their Anglia range) had a capacity of 997 cc and overhead valves. It was the rarest of all the series of 4/4s, since it went out of production in the following year.
1961	Series IV introduced, powered by a 1340 cc ohv Ford engine (as used in the Consul Classic).
1963	Series V introduced powered by Ford 1500 cc Cortina engine. Shortly afterwards a Series V Competition model became available, using the Cortina GT engine.
1968	Introduction of the 4/4 1600. 4/4 four-seater available for first time since 1950 (in the meantime all four-seaters had been Plus 4s).
1969	Body widened bringing the width at the windscreen up to the same size as on the Plus 8.

The Morgan Sports Car Club of Great Britain

Four-wheeler lovers in Britain join the Morgan Sports Car Club, which was founded in 1951 and now has almost 1,500 members. As with all the other clubs its activities comprise competitions, technical assistance and social activities.

(Above) The club's most important annual event is the National Meeting. The first one, MOG 1, was held at Mount Pocono, Pennsylvania, in 1971 and that remained the venue for MOGs 2, 3, 4 and 5. In 1976 the meeting was transferred to Luray, Virginia. This picture of MOG 3 taken in July 1973 gives some idea of the enthusiasm generated at these meetings.

(Right) Commemorative metal plaques like this one are given to all who attend the National Meetings.

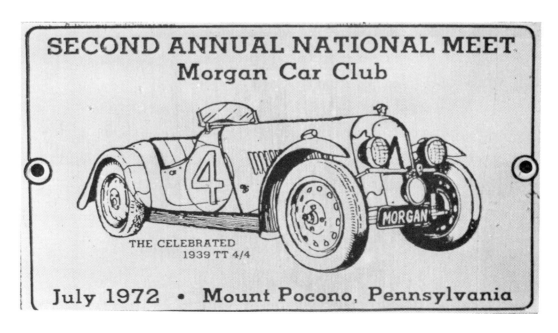

SECOND ANNUAL NATIONAL MEET
Morgan Car Club

THE CELEBRATED
1939 TT 4/4

July 1972 • Mount Pocono, Pennsylvania

(Above) The Morgan Car Club's banner is here seen reflected in the disc of a 1953 flat rad at MOG 5.

(Top left) The Morgan Car Club of Washington DC on its Autumn Tour of Burkeville, Virginia, in September 1974. Photographed at the farm of Dr. John Seem.

(Bottom left) Club members from Richmond, Virginia on their Spring Tour in April 1975 at Bryant Park.

The Morgan Sports Car Club, Washington DC

(Left) A touch of glamour at MOG 5: Miss Lois Norris of Alexandria, Virginia, the owner of a 1965 4/4 Series V, in her MOG 5 T-shirt.

One distinct advantage American Mog-owners have over the rest of us is that they can get themselves an appropriate number plate.

Number plate borrowed from the car of a leading Dallas Mog-owner.

Mort Kuff's 4/4 photographed by Tony Marchetti and Edwin Atkins.

175

The Morgan Owners' Club of Australia

As Morgans have been imported into Australia since long before the war, it is scarcely surprising to find a highly enthusiastic and long-established club in that continent. The MOCA was founded in August 1958 by Ken Ward and initially had only about ten members. By 1976 the number had reached 126 and the Club was based on two centres, one in Victoria and one in New South Wales. An annual inter-state rally is organised and an annual summer camping holiday. Both centres hold regular monthly meetings and all members are kept in touch by the monthly magazine, *The Morgan Ear*. Numerous competitions are also organised with other clubs which, like the MOCA, are affiliated to the Confederation of Australian Motor Sport.

The cars in this photograph constitute one-thirteenth of the total production of Plus-4-Plusses. (For details of this model, see the chapter 'Some Very Rare Models'.)
(Geoff Margetts)

A poster produced in 1976 for the Newcastle Morgan agents.
(*Watts Collection*)

A Morgan Le Mans Replica, 1939. This very rare machine was for many years the property of Mr. Pritchard, a founder member of the Morgan Sports Car Club. Its Coventry Climax engine is here revealed at the Morgan 60th Anniversary Meeting at Prescott in 1970. (Full details of the Le Mans Replica are given in the chapter 'Some Very Rare Models'.)
(Dixon Smith)

Chris Cooke's Modsports 4/4 with rear-mounted radiator. (Full details of this car are given in the chapter 'Modsports, Prodsports, and other recent successes'.)

(Peter Pearce)

In a continent the size of Australia, communications always pose a problem. For MOCA, this has been overcome to a great extent by the monthly *Morgan Ear*, which has been produced since 1966.

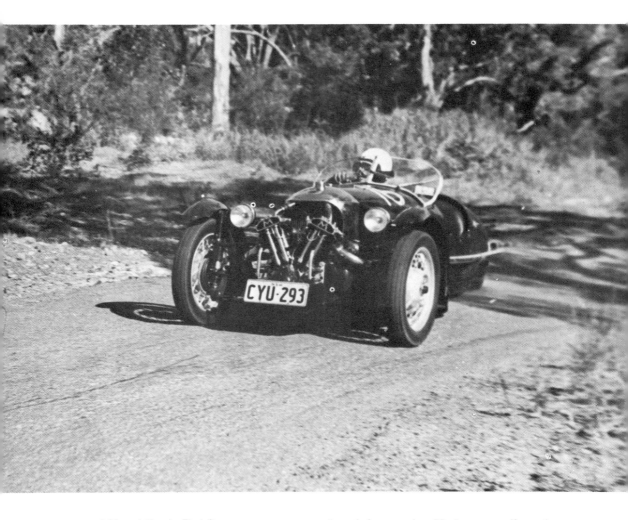

(Above) Ernie Dal Santo—a very popular club captain. He has contributed a great deal towards organising interesting runs for the club—drawing on his excellent knowledge of the countryside. He is pictured here in his 1937 MX4 at Amaroo: three-wheeler lovers should remember that the last V-twins ever made by the factory—one batch of one dozen assembled just after the war—were all sent to Australia, where they did much to enhance the reputation of the marque.

(Right) Ken Ward, founder and current vice-president, in his Plus 4—one of the many Morgans he owns. Since 1960 Ken and his brother have been the Morgan agents for New South Wales.

178

(*Above*) Line up at the first inter-state rally of the MOCA, held in January 1969 at Narrandera, New South Wales. Thirty-six cars attended the event, although only eight of these were Morgans.

(*Below*) The Morgan down under.
(*MTWC*)

The Morgan Sports Car Club of France

The President of the Morgan Sports Car Club of France, Patrick Boisvieux, and his wife with their 1971 4/4 1600.

M. Boisvieux founded the French club in 1973, since when it has gathered new members at a rate of twenty to thirty per year. M. Boisvieux is responsible for Western France while Yvon Alsamora runs the Toulouse group. Local meetings are arranged quite regularly and there is an annual national meeting. But, says Patrick, 'The French are too selfish to attend such meetings in great numbers for reasons of their own!'

Morgan·Club Deutschland

The Morgan-Club Deutschland was born when a number of German Morgan owners met at Frankfurt in October 1973, the first president being Nick Börsch. He was succeeded in 1973 by the present president, Pius Kuhlmann. In 1974 the MCD became an officially registered club with a president, a vice president and four department heads, each covering a different area. Membership is now in the sixties and attendance at the important meetings tends to be very good.

(Top right) A club gathering in a sunny meadow at Heidenheim (near Stuttgart) in May 1976. Note the splendid headgear.

(Bottom right) Ewald Vormann working on his Plus 8 after a crash in East Germany. As with all the clubs, maintenance and restoration are an important part of the life of the MCD.

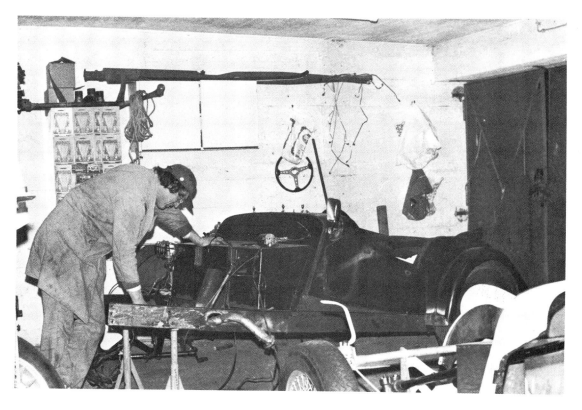

(Left) The Morgan Cup presented to the MCD in commemoration of the visit of Peter and Jane Morgan to Berlin in 1975.

(Below) A meeting at a *biergarten* in Heidenheim. Here, in the shadow of the lime trees, drivers were able to drink the special wheat beer produced in that region.

Club president Pius Kuhlmann with his Plus 8 during a rebuild.

Sixty Morgans parked in the courtyard of a monastery near Riedenburg in September 1975. The monks brew their own cloister beer on the premises, which the drivers found very much to their taste.

The Morgan Sports Car Club, Holland

The Morgan Sports Car Club, Holland, was founded by two enthusiasts in April 1972. Membership is now approaching a total of seventy, of whom three-quarters are either Morgan owners or else have a Morgan on order.

Two main meetings are organised every year: in the spring and the autumn. As the government does not allow races or sprints and as there are no hills to climb in Holland, these meetings comprise touring, driving tests and an excellent dinner. As Holland is such a small country, all the club members know each other very well and form a close group.

Cars lined up for the driving tests at the MSCH spring meeting in 1975. The erect hoods give an indication of what the weather was like that day.

After the tests, the competitors wait in the yard of a local farm for the prize-giving.

The 1976 spring meeting attracted a very good turnout and gave this herd of Fresian cows something to think about.

The Morgan Owners' Group of Sweden

The idea of forming a club in Sweden first came up in the spring of 1966 when Arne Holmstrom met Anders Engstrom. But it was not until 1967 that the idea was really put into practice. The first meeting was held in January that year, and was attended by the total club membership of six. From that small start the club has blossomed and flourished until it now has almost fifty members. Its activities include hill climbs, gymkhanas and rallies and it has organised a number of expeditions to England. Sometimes it joins forces with other clubs in its competitive events, such as the Swedish Austin-Healey and M.G. Clubs, and the Morgan-Club Deutschland.

(Left) From 1968 to 1972 (when the track became unusable because of the condition of the surface), the Club organised very successful annual hill-climbs at Omberg. The hill is 1,100 metres long and has a gradient of one in ten. A handicap system was introduced to give everyone a fair chance. Here some of the cars may be seen in the paddock at Omberg in 1971. The cars in this picture range from a 1952 Plus 4 to a 1969 Plus 8.
(Gunnar Andersson)

(Above) Anders Engstrom's 1954 Plus 4 half-way up the hill at Omberg.
(Gunnar Andersson)

The visit of the Swedish Club to the Morgan factory in 1967. On the same trip
they visited the BRM factory, the Montagu Motor Museum, Prescott and
many other places of interest.
(Gunnar Andersson)

The Morgan Owners' Group's stand at the Sports Car Show in Stockholm in
March 1976. The piper is not a member!
(Lennart Johansson)

The New Factory

In the autumn of 1972, feeling that the main factory was somewhat crowded, Peter Morgan acquired the neighbouring factory. Although part of it is let to another firm, this has increased Morgan's floor space by 12,000 square feet.

The later stages of production are now carried out inside the new factory. Cars are fitted with their basic trim (i.e. the inside trim less seats and carpets). Hoods and tonneaux are assembled and fitted to the cars to which they belong, together with seats and carpets. In the final finish area, side screens, hoods, bonnet catches, door handles, windscreens and other items are fitted. Finally, the cars' electrical systems are wired up—then all that remains is the road test.

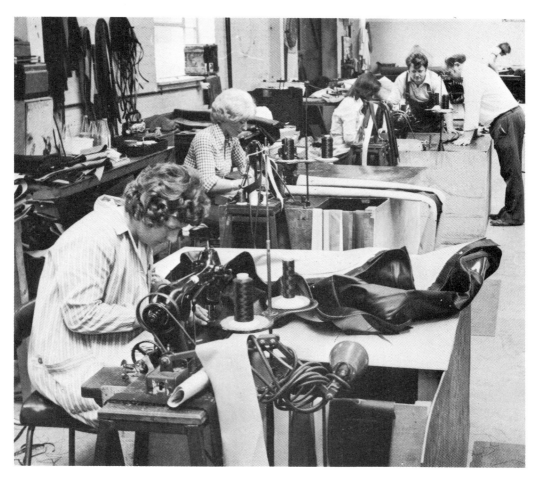

(Above) Part of the area used for hood making.

(Top left) Inside there is an impression of brightness and spaciousness.

(Bottom left) The area used for wiring up the instruments, etc., for the final finish and final test.

Although most Morgan seats come ready-made from outside suppliers, if a customer requires reclining seats or leather trim, the work is carried out here in the new factory. The seat squab for the Standard 4/4 is also made here, although not many cars are fitted with it now.

... and Two Vital Features Rarely Seen

Not a beautiful lily pond but the vital Auxiliary Fire-Fighting Equipment installed at the government's request at the rear of the factory during the last war. It is now well stocked with fish which the factory staff feed with crumbs from their sandwiches in the lunch hour. This flattering picture does not reveal the true nature of the auxiliary FFE—it is in fact just a large, circular, open-topped metal tank.

The bright colours of the gleaming new cars parked in the despatch bay never failed to attract large numbers of birds into this part of the factory. And of course, no self-respecting bird likes to fly round for very long without leaving a calling-card. The problem was a serious one and seemingly intractable, until in the mid-sixties, someone thought of leaving a stuffed owl on guard. This particular bird—an absolutely genuine owl and no imitation—was found in a house near Malvern. Since his installation in the despatch bay, there has not been a single disaster. No bird has the courage to enter now.

Modsports, Prodsports and Other Successes

The Morgan was a born winner. In 1910 it astonished the cyclecar world by outstripping all other makes at Brooklands. Now, nearly seventy years later, it is still outstripping all rivals in its class. In this chapter, we look at some of the men—and the cars—who have been responsible for the most significant recent successes.

Modsports

Modified sports car racing has become tremendously popular in recent years. The car must use the same kind of engine as is normally used by the manufacturer, also the same gearbox, rear axle and method of suspension. Beyond that, extensive modification is allowed.

Chris Cooke is a keen Modsports Morgan fanatic, who has devoted all his energies to the 4/4. His beautiful machine is illustrated in the colour section of this book. Unfortunately, the combination of a job that is always keeping him abroad during the racing season, a crash and various technical problems have restricted his degree of success. Nevertheless, he has shown what can be done with plenty of enthusiasm and imagination.

Cooke bought his car from Rob Wells of Libra Motive in London and began to race early in 1975. Out of 13 starts he achieved two overall seconds, was twice second in his class, and wound up third in the BARC Modsports championship (up-to-two-litre class). He has also twice scored the fastest time of the day at hill climbs.

Modsports, Prodsports and other successes

Chris Cooke at the wheel of his Modsports 4/4.
(*Ernest Cooke*)

The car is equipped with a space frame—a superstructure of tubes to keep the chassis rigid and incorporating the roll bar. To compensate for the rigidity of the chassis, he has increased the travel on the front suspension to $4\frac{1}{2}$ inches using a different kind of shock-absorber mounting and Spax shockers. It is powered by an 1800 cc Ford-Cosworth engine equipped with D.F.V. formula I pistons, a steel crankshaft, special con-rods and a special cylinder head made by Johnny Middleton of Competition Engines.

The body is made of fibreglass with an aluminium bonnet. He has fitted 9·2 inch tyres on ten inch rims at the front, and 10·2 inch tyres on 12 inch rims at the rear.

Following an RAC decision to ban fly-screens from 1st January 1976, Chris decided to compensate for the loss of speed caused by adding a windscreen. He therefore moved the radiator to the space normally occupied by the spare wheel, leaving only a wind-proof dummy grille at the front. This has improved both the wind flow and the weight distribution of the car. With him in the cockpit the car weighs 12 cwt: $6\frac{1}{4}$ on the front and $5\frac{3}{4}$ on the rear.

Prodsports

Production sports car racing imposes very strict limitations on what modifications may be carried out. The cars are thus very close indeed to the models normally produced by their manufacturers. This kind of racing has proved extremely popular.

The name that first comes to mind when Prodsports is mentioned is that of Chris Alford. In 1975, driving as a member of the John Britten Racing Team, he entered fifteen BRSCC Prodsports races, his class being for cars costing from £1,400 to £2,500. The result was that he won his class in *all* of them, and was the outright winner of the Championship. This 100 per cent victory rate is something that will never be forgotten by the Morgan world. In many of the races, his lead when taking the chequered flag was as much as 15-20 seconds. The very fast straights of Silverstone and Mallory Park caused him a little more anxiety, although he says that these were also the most satisfying of all the races.

1975 was Chris Alford's first year driving a Morgan. His previous experience had been gained chiefly in Formula Ford in which he raced extensively from 1969 to 1974. Speaking of the Morgan, he says, 'It is great fun and very easy to drive. In fact it's very easy to overdrive which means you have to slow yourself down a bit because moving sideways all the time is rather slow.'

The racing engine was prepared by Dave Minister. It gave Chris no trouble at all, even though he frequently revved it right off the clock. In fact throughout the whole season, the car was 100 per cent reliable.

On twelve occasions during 1975, the car set the fastest lap time of the day and currently holds six lap records.

The grin of a champion—Chris Alford in his supremely successful 4/4.

(Left) Chris Alford in action on 13th July 1975 at Brand's Hatch. This was a typical result: he won his class, came third overall and took the lap record in 63·6 seconds
(Fred Scatley)

The 1975 Land's End Trial

Since the very earliest days of the company, Morgans have done consistently well in the Motor Cycle Club's Lands End Trial. The event no longer has the same significance or importance which it enjoyed in earlier years. Nevertheless, it still draws the crowds and has an enthusiastic following. In view of this, Morgan lovers cannot fail to feel rather proud that the three works cars entered in the 1975 run all won first-class awards—with the result that Morgans won the team prize.

(Opposite) The three works cars in the 1975 Land's End Trial. In the distance, towards the right and approaching Blue Hills Mine, are Geoff Margetts and A. T. Hall in a 1969 4/4. In the middle are Jim Goodall and his wife in his early Plus 8, and in the foreground in the prototype Plus 8 are Maurice Owen and Basil de Mattos.
(Paul Salmon)

(Left) Owen and de Mattos on a tricky section of Blue Hills Mine. That prototype Plus 8 is still going beautifully. *(Paul Salmon)*

Racing the Plus 8

Chris Lawrence has always been famed for his remarkable skill in tuning Morgans. When Brian Haslam wanted his Plus 8 tuned up in 1972, it was to Lawrence that he brought it. Chris found the Buick-Rover engine far harder to improve than the old Plus 4 Triumph engine: the design imposed severe restrictions on what could be achieved without embarking on tremendously complex and therefore expensive modifications. Nevertheless, he did his best, suffering a number of setbacks on the way. His initial problem was that when he got the engine to go, it blew itself up all too easily; yet when it was below the point of blowing up, it was too slow.

After experimenting with conversions of his own design, Lawrence imported an Iskenderian conversion kit from Los Angeles. This kit, which comprised camshafts, pistons, etc., turned out well. He then designed his own exhaust system and battled with different kinds of ignition, finally selecting the Lucas Opus system. Moreover he bored out the engine to about 3,800 cc. All these modifications were beginning to have some significant effect on the car when, in 1973, Haslam had the misfortune to drop it off its trailer whilst going up a hill. The machine was virtually written off. Lawrence bought the remains, and had the car rebuilt, fitting new camshafts, lifters, valve springs and push-rods from Racer Brown. After this treatment, the car went better than ever, and in Robin Gray. Lawrence found a driver capable of making the most of its abilities.

Brought up on motorcycle and Ford Escort racing, Robin first drove a Morgan in 1972 and finished second his first time out at Mallory Park. 'The Morgan was very easily driveable after what I had been used to,' he says; 'it was a car I slotted into immediately and drove straight off. Sometimes I think it is the closest possible thing to a four-wheeler motor cycle. It calls for a "seat of pants" driving technique.'

During 1973 he began to race the car somewhat irregularly. Yet even so, he came third in the unlimited class of the Modified Sports Car Championship.

Modsports, Prodsports and other successes

During the winter of 1973, in co-operation with Chris Lawrence, he modified the suspension, fitted larger tyres (9 inch front, 10 inch rear) and brought the engine's power up to 280 bhp. As a result, he won his class in the 1974 BARC championship. But this was no flash in the pan: in 1975 he not only won his class in the BARC Modsports championship, but came second in the BRSCC modsports series held in the Midlands. Indeed he was leading the series for some time and might well have won if a number of dates had not clashed with BARC meetings. Of his 22 starts in 1975, Robin scored 13 wins. Five of these were outright wins and five were class wins.

Robin Gray in a BARC Modsports race at Snetterton in the spring of 1975. He won a new lap record for his class.
(Fred Scatley)

On three wheels again—this time at Silverstone in 1976.
(*J. St. J. Bloxham*)

(*Left*) Robin Gray's prospects for 1976 seemed very promising when he had a
serious crash early in the season. Happily he was not hurt. Here he is seen (*left*)
with Chris Lawrence (*right*) and the remains of their car shortly after the crash.

In recent years, the Plus 8 has frequently been seen at Prodsport as well as Modsport events. Here, John Britten is seen driving in the 1975 BRSCC Production Sports Car Championship. Out of eleven starts, during the year, John scored three wins, five seconds, and two thirds, and finished up second in his class (fourth overall) in the Championship.

(Right) Another regular Plus 8 competitor in Modsport racing is Charles Morgan, seen here about to climb into his car at Silverstone. The registration number of this car will be familiar to many—it belongs to the second prototype Plus 8, which is still going as well as ever.
(John Britten)

The Art of Don Jellyman

Don and Cecily Jellyman are both artists and Morgan lovers. He has a recent Plus 8; she has a 4/4 Series II. No one has captured the spirit and humour of the Morgan world more aptly than Don.

'No good wearing out the Moggie in a race like this.'

Morgan in the space age.

"Map Reference correct.   Just the old usual London Centre
Noggin and Natter."

(Below) 'The Regulations quite clearly state — no tops will be worn.'

One of the major problems that Morgan's chief designer Maurice Owen had to overcome when building the prototype Plus 8 was how to fit the carburettors under the bonnet. This was how Don saw the problem.

"Oh well, back to the drawing-board."

Index

By the same author—and from the same publishers—the only comprehensive
history of the marque: 'Morgan: First and Last of the Real Sports Cars'.